LINDSAY BARRETT GEORGE

In the Woods: Who's Been Here?

Greenwillow Books, New York

It is cool and sunny on this autumn afternoon. The smell of sweet fern is everywhere.

"William, do you want to go for a walk?" asks Cammy.

"Sure," says William. "Let's go."

The children follow a well-worn path
into the woods.
They walk under an old cherry tree.
They see an empty nest.

Who's been here?

A northern oriole.

Cammy and William come to a big rock. A tree has split it apart, and a flat stone juts out of the tree.

Who's been here?

A red squirrel.

The trail follows an old stone wall.
The children and their dog, Sam,
climb over it.
A clump of milkweed plants grows in
the field on the other side.
Something hangs from a milkweed leaf.

Who's been here?

A monarch butterfly.

Cammy and William climb over a smooth gray tree that has fallen across the trail. The bark has been gnawed off the branches close to the ground.

Who's been here?

A snowshoe hare.

Cammy finds a blue feather on the trail.
Then she finds another one on a leaf
and five more under a laurel bush.

Who's been here?

A goshawk
and a blue jay.

Gray rock breaks up the leaf-covered hillside.
Something black catches the children's eyes. It is a small, dark cave.
Sam runs ahead and barks at the opening.
William stops and grabs his sister's hand.
There are bleached bones on the ledge outside the cave.

Who's been here?

A family of
red foxes and
a woodchuck.

William and Cammy stop beside a large gray boulder.
Something strange is stuck to the rock.

Who's been here?

A mud dauber.

An orange wood lily stands in a sunny clearing. The flower is almost as tall as Cammy.

There is another stalk next to it. But the flower is gone.

Who's been here?

A deer.

Cammy and William follow the path
on their way home. The rich smell of
sweet fern fills the air again.
They find a basket on a blanket under
an old apple tree.
"I wonder who's been here?" William asks.
But Cammy knows. . . .

The **northern (Baltimore) oriole**, an insect eater, migrates north in the spring to mate, build its nest, and raise its young. The oriole weaves its pouch-like nest in the outer branches of willows, wild cherry, and American elm trees. Here it is safe from tree-climbing snakes, raccoons, and opossums.

The **goshawk** is a fast and fearless hawk that hunts other birds. A goshawk will catch a bird like the blue jay in the air. Holding its victim in its sharp talons, the hawk then drops to the ground for the kill.

The **red squirrel** is smaller, faster, and shyer than its familiar gray cousin. The tiny, rich seeds found in pinecones are its favorite food. A chickadee, searching for insects in the bark of a hemlock tree, watches as the red squirrel eats.

Male and female **foxes** share the job of rearing and guarding their young, which are born in the spring. A woodchuck brought to the den will be eaten by the parents and cubs, and its bones will become playthings for the young foxes.

The **monarch butterfly**'s life cycle centers on the milkweed plant. Its eggs are laid on the milkweed's stems. When a caterpillar hatches from an egg, it feeds on the milkweed leaves, then hangs from them as it transforms itself into a chrysalis. In about ten days it emerges as a butterfly, leaving the empty chrysalis behind.

The **mud dauber** is a kind of wasp. The female mud dauber uses mud to build a nest that looks like a row of tubes. Then the female finds a spider and paralyzes it with a poisonous sting, stuffs the spider into one of the tubes, and lays an egg on it. When the egg hatches, the wasp larva eats the paralyzed spider.

The **snowshoe hare**'s fur is white in winter and brown in summer. In winter it eats the bark and twigs of trees and shrubs and the new growth of spruce and other pine trees. The hare's large feet help it run on top of the snow.

The **deer** are in their summer coats, which are soft, short, and bright. This graceful doe (female deer) is nipping off the flowering top of a rare wood lily.

For Bill, who showed me the forest and the trees

Special thanks to Nathan Cerato, Ted Sokolowski, and Aspen

Gouache paints were used for the full-color art. The text type is Usherwood Medium.
Copyright © 1995 by Lindsay Barrett George
All rights reserved. No part of this book may be reproduced or utilized in any form or by any means, electronic or mechanical, including photocopying, recording, or by any information storage and retrieval system, without permission in writing from the Publisher, Greenwillow Books, a division of William Morrow & Company, Inc., 1350 Avenue of the Americas, New York, NY 10019.
Printed in Singapore by Tien Wah Press
First Edition   10 9 8 7 6 5 4 3 2 1

Library of Congress Cataloging-in-Publication Data
George, Lindsay Barrett.
In the woods: who's been here? / Lindsay Barrett George.
    p.   cm.
Summary: A boy and girl in the woods find an empty nest, a cocoon, gnawed bark, and other signs of unseen animals and their activities.
ISBN 0-688-12318-X (trade).   ISBN 0-688-12319-8 (lib. bdg.)
1. Animals—Juvenile literature.   [1. Animals—Habits and behavior.]
I. Title.   QL49.G45   1995   591—dc20   93-16244   CIP   AC